A **THINKING** *of* **OTHERS** BOOK

Book One — Cherishing Others

Tessa's Treasures

Written by

Gary Bower

Illustrated by

Jan Bower

Edited by Anthony Weber

Storybook Meadow

Traverse City, Michigan

ACKNOWLEDGMENTS

My deepest gratitude goes to those who have contributed to the making of this book.
To the Author of everything good, for His inspiration, guidance, and grace.
To our children for their input and for carrying a heavier share of the household responsibilities.
To Anthony for making his exceptional editing skills available to us.
To our friends at Church of the Living God for their prayers and encouragement.

- Gary Bower

I wish to thank my close friends, Deb Pianki and Jackie Kaschel, and my dear brother, Pete Norris, whose encouraging words during this project were more appreciated than they could possibly know. My thanks also goes to Tynae Bower and Louis Kennedy. What wonderful little subjects to paint!

- Jan Bower

Tessa's Treasures
Text copyright © 2000 by Gary D. Bower
Illustrations copyright © 2000 by Jan Bower

Published by Storybook Meadow Publishing
7700 Timbers Trail, Traverse City, Michigan 49684

Edited by Anthony Weber

Library of Congress Card Number: 00-192257

ISBN 0-9704621-0-7

Printed and bound in Canada

In loving memory of
Michael David Bower
who wisely pursued true treasures.

Tessa watched as her friend, Luke, played with his dinosaurs. "Rrrraarrr!" he said, pretending to make a big dinosaur eat a smaller one.

"You can't guess what I have," Tessa teased.

Luke looked up. "Whatcha got?"

"Oh, just something."

"Can I see it?"

"Nope."

"How come?"

"Because."

"But I just want to see it."

Tessa shook her head. "It's a secret."

"Please?"

"Nope."

Luke frowned. "That's not fair," he pouted.
"I let you see my dinosaurs."

Tessa thought about that. "Well...okay," she told
him, "but you can't touch it." She opened her hands
a tiny crack to let Luke have a peek. It was a red
toy ring. Quickly, Tessa pulled her hands back.

"I'm going to put it in my treasure box," she
announced. She got up and skipped across the
room to a shoe box that sat on the floor. Lifting
the lid, she gently placed the ring inside. Then
she picked up the box and hugged it tightly.

"These are my treasures," she said proudly.
"Do you have any treasures, Luke?"

"Are dinosaurs treasures?"

"No," said Tessa. "Dinosaurs are ugly."

"I like 'em," said Luke.

After Luke and his dinosaurs went home, Tessa opened her box again and admired her treasures. Along with her ring were two long beaded necklaces, a pretty piece of driftwood that she had found at the beach, three shiny dimes, some butterfly stickers that the dentist gave her, and one of Mother's old watches that didn't work anymore.

"I like these treasures," she said to herself. "They're nice. Much nicer than some ugly old dinosaurs."

The next day was Tuesday. It was raining when Luke came over that morning, so the children stayed inside and drew pictures with markers. Tessa drew a colorful rainbow. Luke drew a big, hairy spider.

"Do you like my rainbow?" Tessa asked.

"I guess so," said Luke.

She smiled. "You can have it."

"Thanks. How do you like my picture?"

Tessa crinkled up her nose. "It's a spider."

"Yep," said Luke.

"But spiders are creepy," Tessa pointed out.

Luke shrugged his shoulders. "I like 'em," he said. "Do you want it?"

"Well...okay," Tessa decided. She folded the spider picture neatly and put it in her treasure box. Luke stuffed the rainbow picture in his pocket.

After lunch the sun came out, and Tessa's mother said they could play in the pool. They laughed and splashed so hard that Tessa got thirsty, so Luke helped her get a drink.

"Hey, look at that," said Luke, pointing at something on the ground. He picked it up.

"It's just a stone," Tessa said. She had seen lots of stones before.

"It's a *Petoskey** stone," he added. "See how pretty it looks when it gets wet?"

Tessa had never seen a Petoskey stone. Luke handed it to her. She turned the stone in her hand, looking at its pretty designs. Luke could tell that she liked it.

"Do you want to keep it?" he asked.

Tessa's eyes sparkled. "Sure!" she said. "I'll put it in my treasure box."

**The Petoskey stone is the state stone of Michigan. These Northern Michigan stones are polished and used to make beautiful jewelry.*

On Wednesday, they played with clay.

"Look at me!" said Luke. A large blob of red clay covered his nose. Under his nose hung a white clay moustache.

"I'm a grandpa!" he said in an old voice.

Tessa laughed when she saw him. "You need some white eyebrows, Grandpa," she said with a grin. She began rolling out long pieces of white

clay on the table.

"Those look like snakes," said Luke.

Tessa dropped her hands into her lap. "Snakes are gross," she said.

"I like 'em," Luke replied. He peeled the clay from his nose. "Do you want to keep my red nose?"

Tessa made a strange face. "That's not a treasure," she said. Luke just looked at her. He wasn't smiling. When he didn't say anything, she changed her mind.

"Well...alright." So she put it in her treasure box.

On Thursday, the children went to the creek to look for more treasures. Tessa picked some pretty pink flowers. Luke found a frog.

"Hey, Luke! Would you like to smell my flowers?" Tessa asked.

Luke didn't hear her. He was busy with his frog.

"Look what I found!" he said. He held the frog up to Tessa's face.

"Yuck!" she said, backing away. She didn't want the frog to jump on her.

"What's the matter?" asked Luke.

"Frogs are slimy," Tessa said.

"I like 'em," said Luke.

Tessa decided to take her flowers home and put them in her treasure box. Luke was going to put the frog in his pocket, but he thought that it might get squished, so he let it go.

Luke didn't come over on Friday. He had a fever.

Tessa played all by herself that day. She dressed up in some old clothes that her mother kept in a wooden chest.

These must be mother's treasures, she thought.

As she played, she noticed that the house seemed quieter than usual. Whenever Luke came over, the house was always full of lots of giggling and dinosaur noises.

"Oh, well," she told herself, "Luke probably wouldn't want to play dress up, anyway."

Luke was sick on Saturday, too. Tessa played dress up all alone again, but it wasn't fun anymore. Looking for treasures wasn't fun either. Nothing was fun all by herself. Luke was always fun, even if he did like creepy, slimy things.

On Sunday, Tessa looked for Luke at church, but he wasn't there. She missed him.

That night at bedtime, Tessa was sorting through her treasures. She unfolded the picture that Luke had given her. *It actually looks quite nice,* she thought...*for a spider.* She held the Petoskey stone that Luke had found. It wasn't wet anymore, so it looked dull instead of shiny. She tried to pick up Luke's red clay nose, but it crumbled in her hand. Then she saw something that made her very sad. The flowers she had picked by the creek were all dried up and dead. She felt like crying.

Knock, knock. Daddy was at her door. "Any new treasures today, Princess?" he asked as he sat on the edge of her bed.

"No," said Tessa.

Daddy prayed with her and gave her a hug. When he stood up to leave, Tessa said, "Daddy?"

"What is it, Honey?"

"My flowers died."

Daddy slowly sat back down. "Oh? I'm sorry," he said. "But, you can't expect flowers to last forever, Tessa. Most things don't, you know."

"They didn't last very long at all," Tessa said. "Maybe I shouldn't put flowers in my treasure box."

"There are plenty of flowers by the creek," Daddy pointed out. "You can always pick more."

Tessa looked very thoughtful. Daddy could tell that she wanted to ask him a question.

"What is it, Princess?"

"Daddy, how can I tell if something is a treasure?"

Daddy's eyes sparkled brightly. "Tessa," he said tenderly, "**when you find something that you care about very much, something that you never want to lose, and something so special that it can never be replaced...** *then you've found a treasure.*"

Tessa was quiet for a moment. Finally, she asked, "Do you have any treasures, Daddy?"

Daddy kissed her forehead softly. "Oh, yes," he whispered.

On Monday morning, Luke came over to play again. He was feeling much better.

"Weren't you bored with no one to play with?" Tessa asked.

"I don't know," he replied. "I guess so. But yesterday I got a new puppy."

Tessa's eyes grew big. "Wow!" she said. "I like puppies. They're cute. Not like spiders and frogs. They're creepy and slimy."

"Yeah, but I still like 'em," Luke said with a shrug. Then he looked at Tessa's treasure box. "Hey, did you look for any new treasures?" he asked.

"Maybe."

"Well, did you find any?"

"One."

"Lemme see it!" Luke said. But when he reached for the box, Tessa pulled it away.

"Nope," she teased.

"How come?"

"Because."

"Please?"

"Nope."

"That's not fair," said Luke. "I told you about my puppy."

Tessa thought about that. "You're right," she gave in, holding the box out to him. "You can look in my box if you want to." Then she smiled. "But you won't find my new treasure in there."

"Why not?" asked Luke.

"Because..." Tessa giggled,

"...it won't fit!"

"We love because He first loved us."

1 John 4:19

Can you remember?

*What things did Tessa keep in her box
at the beginning of the story?*

*What treasures did Luke give Tessa
or help her find?*

*After just a few days, some things
in Tessa's box didn't seem like
treasures anymore. What were they?*

How many days was Luke sick?

*What special treasure wouldn't fit
in Tessa's box?*

What do you think?

*If you had a treasure box like Tessa's,
what would you put in it?*

How were Luke and Tessa different?

*Can you think of a friend who likes
things that are different from what
you like? What's your friend's name?*

*Why are people more precious
than things?*

*What can you do to show
your friends and family members
how important they are to you?*

A Word from the Author
to
Parents & Teachers

I was sitting in my recliner and reading the sports page, while my younger children played a game on the floor. Suddenly, I had a strange feeling that someone was missing.

"Where's Jasmine?" I asked. I hadn't remembered seeing my five-year-old all evening.

The room grew still. I expected a response from Jan or one of the children, but none came immediately. My eyes slowly scanned the room as I silently did a head count. All the kids wore a puzzled expression. Jan began to snicker.

"I'm right here, Daddy!" came a giggling reply. Jasmine had burrowed through sections of the newspaper, and wormed her way up onto my lap. I had been so caught up in baseball statistics that I hadn't even noticed.

Isn't it funny how the things we are looking for are often right under our noses? Take happiness for instance. In our pursuit of it, who hasn't found himself on an occasional goose chase, going from one possession, accomplishment, or job to another? Like Tessa, sometimes we focus our attention, and even our affection, on items that do not last and are not capable of loving us back. Our "shoe boxes" might be our garages, bank accounts, or credentials. Meanwhile, the true riches of life— relationships with family, friends, and God— have been sitting right there, waiting for us to notice.

My goal in writing Tessa's Treasures was to emphasize this basic truth: *people are more precious than things*. A strong grasp of this fundamental perspective is essential if our children are to experience meaningful lives and lasting relationships. Other healthy character traits such as respect, mercy, honesty, and kindness are much more likely to spring up in a child who has learned to value the lives of others.

One way that you can convey this message to your child is by taking the time to show her that you cherish her more than your hobby, recreational interests, or work. You can further reinforce in her the preciousness of human life by teaching her about the One who left the greatest riches of the universe to pursue a relationship with her. There are many quality Bible story books that can assist you.

It is my sincere hope that Tessa's Treasures will help to produce in your child's heart a greater appreciation for other people.

About the Author & Illustrator

Photo by Christa McCrum

Gary & Jan Bower have been surrounded by children their entire twenty-two years of marriage. They have experienced the miracle of childbirth in four different decades, and have been homeschooling since 1983. Their two sons and nine daughters, ranging from twenty-one years to five months, keep their country home buzzing in Traverse City, Michigan.

In 1999, Gary left a career as a pastor and began writing children's stories, enabling him to be closer to his family. His published writings include stories for *DiscipleLand*, the popular curriculum series for kids produced by Through the Bible Publishers.

Jan has been painting commissioned portraits for more than twenty years. Her medium of choice was oil on canvas for *Tessa's Treasures*, using four-year-old Tynae as a model for Tessa.

All of the Bower children (except baby Kassidy) have contributed to their parents' first book. Some offered helpful editing suggestions or art critiques. Others ran errands, helped with promotion, found a Petoskey stone, drew a rainbow and a spider, assisted Jan in posing her subjects, or took on an extra large share of household duties. Without these amazing children, this book would not have come about.